The Sea Turtles Live On

By Pat Goldys

Chris Wright, Turtle Tracker, who volunteers at the turtle rescue. She taught me all about these wonderful creatures. Now I love sea turtles as much as she does!

Jaymie Reneker, Biologist, provided feedback on story for authenticity.

Thanks, Chris and Jaymie, for the wonderful photos.

Grandma Chris wants to do
Something good for turtles of the sea.
A volunteer at the beach
So a Turtle Tracker she will be!

Grandma Chris walks the beach.
Sees a blob on sand near her feet.
A "Portuguese man of war" is what it is!
A jelly fish, sea turtles love to eat!

She walks steps further
And stumbles upon
A ghost crab peeking!
Sea Turtles, be gone!

Shore Birds are seen
On sand and in sky
Looking for turtles
To take away as they fly.

8

The sandy sea turtles
Run from their nests
Towards the water
To get some rest.

Their nest an upside down light bulb
The eggs like mini ping pong balls
Grandma gets a screened tray
To count the eggs so small.

Some are hatched.
Some are alive.

Some have not hatched.
Some did not survive!

Grandma Chris cares for the turtles.

She keeps watch each and every day.

From the first of May to Halloween Day.

So sea turtles can safely swim away.

ADOPT-A-BEACH
This mile of beach is adopted and cared for by . . .
NSB Turtle Trackers

Only red flashlights shine!

Never have a white light!

To moonlight babies in line!

The red light is just right!

LIGHTS OUT
FOR
SEA TURTLES
NEVER SHINE LIGHTS ON SEA TURTLE NESTS, HATCHLINGS, OR ADULT TURTLES

Break down sand castles.
Beach holes please fill in.
Pick up straws, bags, bottles.
Put in the trash bin.

Grandma Chris was trained
How to rescue turtles in need.
The Marine Science Center brings a bucket.
With sand, salt water and seaweed.

The turtles are taken to the rescue.
Where they are loved and well cared for.
Till the day they are released
To the ocean they adore!

All sea turtle work conducted by trained and permitted individuals under FWC-MTP-162.

If you want to help the sea turtles, go to https://nsbturtles.org/

About the Author

Pat Goldys was born in Baltimore, Maryland and lived there for 63 years. She loves sea turtles and dolphins. She moved to Florida to be near her granddaughter, Mila.

Pat continues to write stories about real events, as well as the make believe. Kids like fiction and nonfiction. She writes stories that kids like to read and parents and grandparents can read to their children.

If you choose to read, please leave a review as I'd love to read your thoughts!